Where Do The Tigers Go?

A collection of children's poetry
by Jack Zager

Published by Luminary Media Group, an imprint of Pine Orchard, Inc.
Visit us on the internet at www.pineorchard.com
Printed in Canada.

ISBN   1-930580-57-6

Yesterday

When I was very young,
I couldn't go out alone.
Had to wait for Brother,
or Mom to get off the phone.

My pup would stand and bark,
or raise his head and moan.
They always opened the door,
but I couldn't go out alone.

Sometimes the rabbits played,
just behind the gate.
I thought I could reach them,
but always was too late.

Things are different now.
I'm not in such a fix.
Now I'm so much older.
You see, I'm nearly six.

Bedtime

Far beyond the daylight
and out into the night,
is the awful darkness,
trying to give me fright.

I pull aside the curtain;
the light goes peeping through,
pale yellow on the grass,
shining on the dew.

I hold on to my bear,
his arm in my hand,
and rub against my eyes
to brush away the sand.

Night is nearly over;
daylight's on the way.
I'm really not alone.
I know my bear will stay.

We creep into the bed,
pull the covers high.
I kiss my bear goodnight
and tell the night goodbye.

Summer Home

If I stood on tiptoe,
I could barely reach the nest,
on a single branch,
apart from all the rest.

At first, three skinny necks
were all that I could see.
But as the days passed by,
they were beautiful to me.

Cheep and peep and flap
and look down at the ground.
Eyes full of wonder
at everything around.

Then one morning early,
before the sun was high,
they teetered on the edge
and soon began to fly.

Summer passed so quickly.
I wanted them to stay.
But when I looked one evening,
all three had flown away.

The nest is empty now,
a sad and lonely place.
But the sound of a cheep
brings a smile to my face.

Vacation Bay

Sunlight glistened brightly.
The wind blew down the beach.
It pushed the waves near,
but kept them out of reach.

I knelt down in the water;
my toes wriggled free.
A little sandy pool
swirled around my knee.

A tiny silver arrow
darted side to side.
It flashed around the pool,
then escaped upon the tide.

I stood and searched the sky.
A graceful wing of white
floated softly downward,
then soared out of sight.

Walking toward the land,
I smiled at the bay.
As long as I remembered,
I'd never be away.

It's Raining

Clouds hung low over the hill
and rain came down in sheets,
turning the ground dark green
and making oil slicks on the streets.

Even the dog was restless,
pacing from door to door.
Finally, he grew bored
and joined me on the floor.

I turned slowly through the pages
of a couple of old books,
and kept asking for the time
until I got some ugly looks.

Finally, the pattering quit.
Some sunshine split a cloud.
The dog went to the door,
barking softly, then quite loud.

We ran into the yard
and watched steam rise off the ground,
then jumped hard as we could
in a puddle we had found.

My clothes turned instant dirty
from the sloppy, muddy spray.
But I really didn't worry
because the sun came out to stay.

Chippy

A tiny nose poked through,
then two bright eyes above.
I saw the little chipmunk.
My heart was filled with love.

He climbed up on the wall
and shook his whiskers dry.
I couldn't stop my laughing,
no matter how I'd try.

His body's short and furry,
a tail that isn't there.
He wrinkles up his forehead
and sniffs the summer air.

I reach out to his head.
He shakes his paws in fright
and flies into his hole.
Now he's out of sight.

I know he'll come again.
He has a lot of pride.
The world belongs to him.
He'll never have to hide.

Halloween

They say it isn't so,
but we all really knew.
When dark came down around us,
the bad we heard was true.

Bats and bears and ghosts,
cat with a nose that twitches.
Those were pretty bad,
but the worst were the witches.

They flew in past a cloud,
screeching on a broom,
zipped right in a window,
and came into your room.

No matter that we're older now,
we still remember the dark,
the howling of the dogs,
and how they'd bay and bark.

It's only a fairy tale.
Anyone will tell you so.
We nod our heads politely
because we really know.

Pup

The sun fell through the window
and lay upon the floor.
It warmed the yellow carpet
and stretched out to the door.

The little dog went after it.
He growled as if to bite.
But no matter how he tried,
it never left his sight.

I laughed at his frustration
and softly held his head.
He dropped upon the carpet
and used it for his bed.

We watched the clouds float over
and quietly douse the light.
It really was the daytime
but could as well been night.

The sun reached out again.
My pup growled with pleasure.
The little joys of life
are the hardest ones to measure.

Pal

My pony was short and fat,
and loved to take a nap.
He'd stand so very still,
his head upon my lap.

If I tried to catch him,
he'd run and buck and kick.
But when you grabbed his mane,
he'd stand just like a stick.

I'd brush and comb his coat
till it glistened in the sun.
But if I tried to ride,
he never thought it fun.

He'd chase the other horses
and eat their food as well.
But he always came to me,
when I rang the feeding bell.

Although I'm much too big
to ride the little guy,
tears came down my cheeks
when we said goodbye.

Where Do the Tigers Go?

Oh, tell me, please do tell me,
I really have to know.
When the night becomes the morning,
where do the tigers go?

I went to bed last evening.
The room was quiet with sound
and standing on the carpet
were tigers all around.

At first, they growled and roared.
I suppose to give me fright.
Then I reached my hand out
and smiled at the sight.

They rolled and purred like kittens.
We laughed and grinned in play.
I told them that I loved them,
but they smiled and crept away.

I've searched throughout the sunshine
and even thought to hide.
For the day is long and lonely
with no tigers by your side.

Long Ago

A little child sits
by the water's splash
and sees a wondrous world
dressed in a scarlet sash.

The sun is setting slowly
over distant road and hill.
But the moving wind is music,
strong and clear and shrill.

The child tilts his head
from side to side,
and hears the magic call
that moves upon the tide.

He has tasted of life's joy
and the seed is planted now
to sprout into a soul
with the mystery of a vow.

I once was such a child,
of hope and curious eye,
whose heart was full of love
to give until I die.

Goodbye

I often walked the path,
watching the birds in the bath,
sitting alone on the grass,
waiting for the sun to pass.

Today I saw her face,
smiling sweetly in my place.
I started to turn away
but her eyes asked me to stay.

We sat side by side on the green,
not really wanting to be seen.
Her eyes large and brown,
the long hair falling down.

At once, we both started to speak.
I, louder, to prove I wasn't meek.
Softly, she touched my hand
and then moved to stand.

"Stay," I heard myself say,
then watched her walk away.
A cold wind blew over me.
Whatever was, was meant to be.

Teens

Sometimes the day turns dim;
I sit beside the chair.
My mind can see him clearly,
his fingers in my hair.

The hands are long and slender
and brush away my sorrow.
I know he isn't real,
but I'll look for him tomorrow.

Vision beautiful and complex,
filled with longing ache.
Even though it's fantasy,
my heart will surely break.

Would I were a woman,
full blown and nearly wild.
Sadly, it's not time yet
and worse, I'm not a child.

Joy of inner feeling,
life is yet to live.
The world will never notice
how much love I have to give.

Date

She is so very pretty.
Eyes, large and soft and round.
Her face is very near,
so I look down at the ground.

We sit upon her couch
and talk about the day.
I'm afraid that if I move,
she'll stand and go away.

She smiles and barely laughs.
I try hard not to blink.
If my friends could see me,
who knows what they'd think!

Girls know how to date.
At least, they say it's so.
But if this is what it's like,
I'm not sure I want to know.

First Love

When I awoke this morning,
the sky was overcast.
I felt a sudden shudder,
a chill that wouldn't last.

I bounded down the stairs
and raced into the street.
The ground was hard and dry
and pushed against my feet.

I looked around the lawns;
the houses were all asleep.
I sat down on the curb
and began to softly weep.

A hand gently touched my hair.
I looked up at his face.
He offered me a smile.
My heart began to race.

We sat and watched the sky.
The sun came shining through.
Our laughter floated upward
and turned the sky to blue.

Hand in hand, we walked.
Our fingers touch in play.
We are so very happy.
It's another lovely day.

About the Author

Jack Zager is a husband, father, and grandfather. He lives in Nashville, Tennessee, where, when he is not writing children's poetry, he is Senior Vice President, Investments with Morgan Stanley.